Junior

Mathst.|||||||||||| 9

Activities for ....eracy

Lesley Higgin

Tarquin

Publisher's Note

Lesley Higgin's tried and tested activities in this volume will enliven hundreds of classrooms and homework sessions across the world.

An experienced teacher and author, she brings practicality and a sense of fun to what can often seem dull learning and reinforcement tasks.

Junior Mathstraks are available in book and ebook form covering ages 7-8, 8-9, 10-11 and Extension for ages 11 and above - as well as this volume.

In addition there are Mathstraks volumes for early Secondary years on Algebra, Geometry and Number.

You can keep up to date with this and other new titles, special offers and more, through registering on our website for our e-mail newsletter or following us on Twitter or Facebook.

Published by Tarquin Publications
Suite 74, 17 Holywell Hill
St Albans
AL1 1DT

www.tarquingroup.com

Distributed in the USA by Parkwest
www.parkwestpubs.com
www.amazon.com & major retailers

Distributed in Australia by OLM www.lat-olm.com.au

Copyright © Lesley Higgin, 2016
Book ISBN: 978-1-907-55078-2
Ebook ISBN: 978-1-911-09328-2

Printed and designed in the United Kingdom

Intoduction

It's always a challenge to be able to provide enough opportunity for children to practise number work, without them getting bored with repetitive exercises. I hope that this book will help.

I have developed the *Mathstraks* series to enable pupils to gain a solid understanding of numeracy through fun, challenge and play.

There are lots of different activities to enable children to use their number skills in a variety of situations, including puzzles, problem-solving and games. I have enjoyed writing the tasks and they have worked extremely well with my classes.

I hope you find the book useful and, most importantly, that the children enjoy it.

Lesley Higgin

Speedy Sums

Each question has an answer which is a mode of transport. First do the calculation, then use the grid below to replace each digit of your answer by a letter.

0	1	2	3	4	5	6	7	8	9
O	S	E	R	C	T	K	I	A	B

1. 297 + 192

answer			
name			

2. 1000 - 517

answer			
name			

3. 903 + 768

answer			
name			

4. 5016 + 4069

answer			
name			

5. 5000 - 165

answer			
name			

6. 3945 + 5817

answer			
name			

7. 53908 - 146

answer				
name				

8. 167999 + 522

answer					
name					

Challenge!

Write addition or subtraction questions to make ARK and ROCKET.

3, 2, 1, ...

A. Use the digits 1, 2, 3 once each in any order to make:

1. An odd number

2. An even number

3. all possible 3-digit numbers

4. the greatest possible 3-digit number

5. the smallest possible 3-digit number.

B. Use your answers to questions 4 and 5 above to answer these questions:

1. Find the difference between the greatest and smallest numbers in part A.

2. Swap the units and hundreds digits in the previous answer.

3. Add your answers to the previous two questions.

C. Repeat section B using the digits 3, 6, 8

D. Now choose your own three digits to repeat section B. All three digits must be different.

Challenge!

Do you get a similar result if you use four digits?

Decimal Sums and Differences

The **sum** of two numbers is found by adding them.

The **difference** of two numbers is found by subtracting the smallest from the largest.

Work out the missing numbers in the following grids like this:

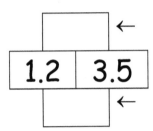

← The sum of the two numbers goes here (4.7)

← The difference of the two numbers goes here (2.3)

1.
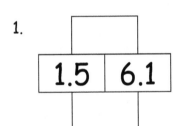

2.
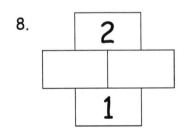

3.
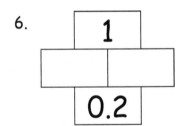

4.
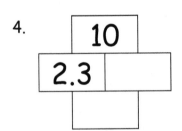

5.

6.

7.
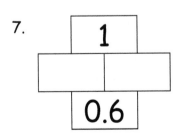

8.

9.
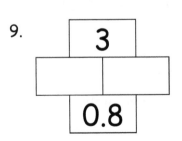

Routes Home

Use the following clues to help each person find their way home.

Write their names where each sequence ends.

- Ed must follow a route starting at 1.2 and adding on 0.2's.

- Jo must follow a route starting at 1.1 and adding on 0.3's.

- Tim must follow a route starting at 2.9 and subtracting 0.3's.

- Amy must follow a route starting at 0.9 and adding on 1's.

- Sue must follow a route starting at 1.5 and adding on 0.4's.

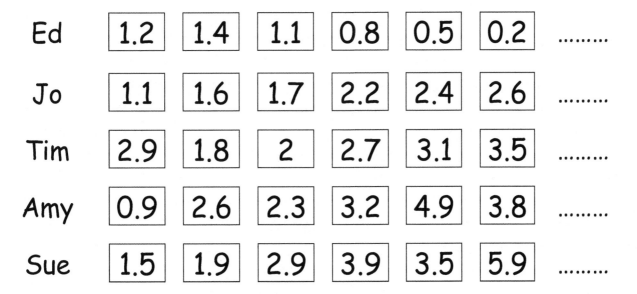

Ed	1.2	1.4	1.1	0.8	0.5	0.2	....
Jo	1.1	1.6	1.7	2.2	2.4	2.6	....
Tim	2.9	1.8	2	2.7	3.1	3.5	....
Amy	0.9	2.6	2.3	3.2	4.9	3.8	....
Sue	1.5	1.9	2.9	3.9	3.5	5.9	....

Challenge!

The starting number in Dave's route is 2.5 and the final number is 4.9. Work out 3 possible sequences which will take Dave home.

Decimal Arrows

Move around the following grids, filling in the answers as you go.

A.   When you move right add 2.6. When you move up add 1.1

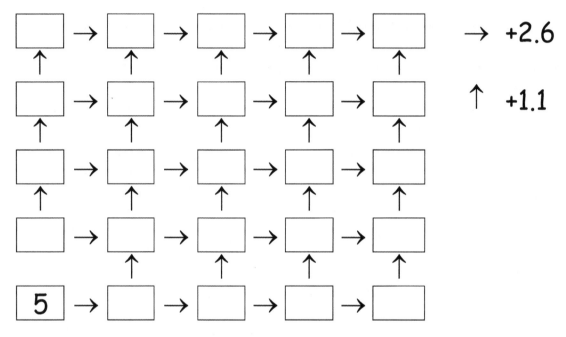

B.   When you move right add 4.5. When you move up add 0.9

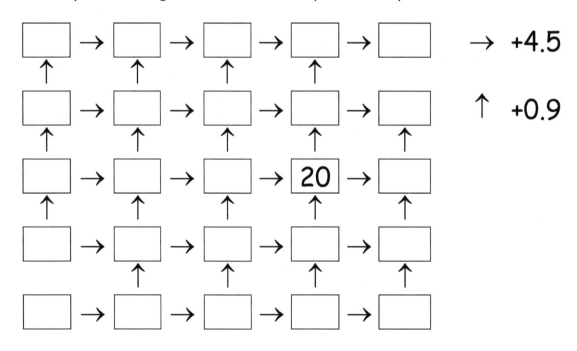

Make a Metre

Cut out the following squares

Match them so that each pair of adjacent sides add to 1 metre.

0.08m	75cm	0.46m
0.5m A 74cm	95cm B 0.22m	0.99m C 0.51m
0.85m	0.3m	0.45m
0.12m	0.04m	0.35m
43cm D 50cm	0.81m E 28cm	49cm F 0.19m
40cm	25cm	0.69m
0.7m	31cm	0.55m
0.26m G 13cm	90cm H 0.05m	0.71m I 0.1m
34cm	92cm	0.88m

Wizard Maze

Sumsgalore the Wizard has to get through the mathematical maze without getting caught by the Terrible Trolls.
Calculate your way around the maze. Only correct answers will lead you to safety!

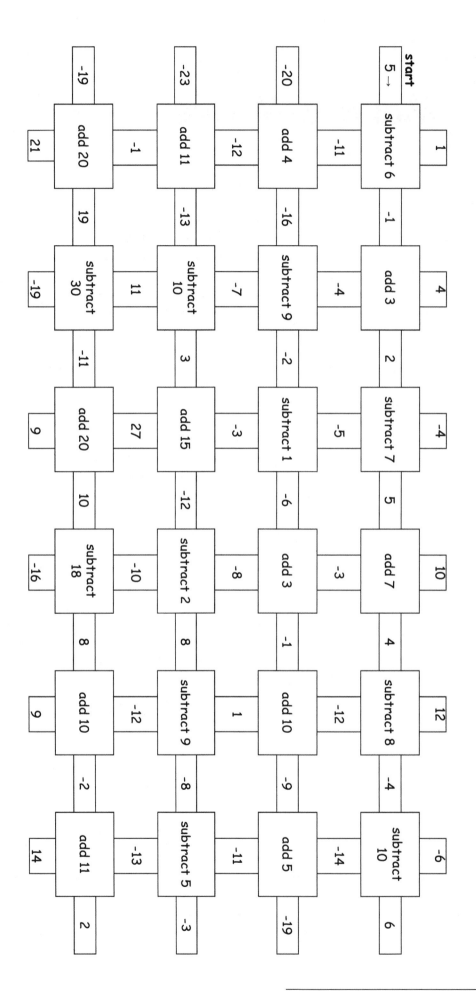

Set the Table

In the following multiplication grids, the numbers 2, 3, 4, 5, 6, 7, 8, 9 have each been used once in the shaded boxes. Work out which number goes where and then complete the rest of the grid.

A.

×				
	42			35
		16		10
	24		36	

B.

×				
	8	6		
			45	
			54	
	32			

C.

×				
	14	18		
				24
			30	18

Challenge!

In C, what do all the numbers inside the grid (not the shaded numbers) have in common?
Why has this happened?

Factor Fiction

- This is a game for 2-3 players. You need counters, a 6-sided dice, paper and pen.

- Start in the centre and take it in turns to throw a 6-sided dice and move your counter in any direction around the board.

- On landing on a square you must name a factor of that number (12 or less). You can then write down that factor.

- If you land on a square and can't write down a factor that you have not already written, then you must cross out your highest factor.

- The winner is the first player to have a complete list of the numbers 1 to 12.

96	36	77	39	40	88	46
23			90			72
49			99			45
87			31			59
24	97	33	1	94	26	91
37			50			36
95			56			60
54			48			13
25	29	44	17	14	63	34

Number Properties

Shade the numbers in the grid according to the following rules:

Factors of 120 shade green

Multiples of 7 shade red

Square numbers shade blue

11	46	68	51	26	38	90	33	27	47	22
31	25	52	70	21	56	41	15	24	10	65
55	64	39	42	76	22	43	2	48	12	34
61	36	53	14	84	63	78	30	80	8	62
32	9	75	23	82	7	13	6	18	3	66
18	16	33	35	77	28	59	40	5	20	23
45	17	37	13	50	72	44	26	19	69	17

Work out all the factors of your answer.

Challenge

There are some numbers which were deliberately left out of the grid, because they could have been shaded more than one colour.

Give some examples of these numbers.

1 to 9 Puzzle

Use the numbers 1, 2, 3, 4, 5, 6, 7, 8, 9 once each in the following spaces to make each calculation correct.

A

$\boxed{} \times \boxed{} \times \boxed{} = 180$

$\boxed{} \times \boxed{} \times \boxed{} = 56$

$\boxed{} \times \boxed{} \times \boxed{} = 36$

B

$\boxed{} \times \boxed{} \times \boxed{} = 64$

$\boxed{} \times \boxed{} \times \boxed{} = 90$

$\boxed{} \times \boxed{} \times \boxed{} = 63$

C

$\boxed{} \times \boxed{} \times \boxed{} = 105$

$\boxed{} \times \boxed{} \times \boxed{} = 24$

$\boxed{} \times \boxed{} \times \boxed{} = 144$

Make a Name

To work out each person's name first do the calculation, then use the grid below to replace each digit of your answer by a letter.

0	1	2	3	4	5	6	7	8	9
O	E	T	D	A	Y	I	S	M	N

1. 421 × 2

answer			
name			

2. 71 × 3

answer			
name			

3. 97 × 5

answer			
name			

4. 67 × 4

answer			
name			

5. 449 × 6

answer				
name				

6. 13 × 16

answer			
name			

7. 157 × 12

answer				
name				

8. 217 × 23

answer				
name				

Challenge!

Work out multiplication questions to make each of the following names:

SAM, MAY, ADA, ANDY, SIMON

Divide Again

Do the division given and write the answer and remainder in the spaces given.

| 35 | ÷ | 4 | = | 8 | remainder | 3 |

Then copy your answer in to the next question space:

| 8 | ÷ | 3 | = | 2 | remainder | 2 |

Repeat the process until you have filled in the whole grid.

1. | 239 | ÷ | 5 | = | | remainder | |
	÷		=		remainder	
	÷		=		remainder	
	÷		=		remainder	

2. | 518 | ÷ | 8 | = | | remainder | |
	÷		=		remainder	
	÷		=		remainder	
	÷		=		remainder	

3. | 2446 | ÷ | 9 | = | | remainder | |
	÷		=		remainder	
	÷		=		remainder	
	÷		=		remainder	

Times Ten

On the following grid, try to find pairs of adjacent numbers where one number is 10 times the other. Connect your pairs of stars with a line.

The lines may be horizontal, vertical or diagonal.

* 0.02	* 0.2	* 0.002	* 2	* 0.2	* 2000	* 2	* 200	* 0.2	* 20	* 0.2	* 2
* 20	* 2	* 2000	* 0.002	* 0.02	* 20	* 0.02	* 200	* 0.02	* 20	* 0.02	* 20
* 200	* 2000	* 0.002	* 2	* 0.2	* 2000	* 0.002	* 2	* 2	* 2000	* 0.2	* 2

What is the answer?

That's an Order!

Put the values in the boxes in order smallest to largest. The corresponding letters should form a mathematical word.

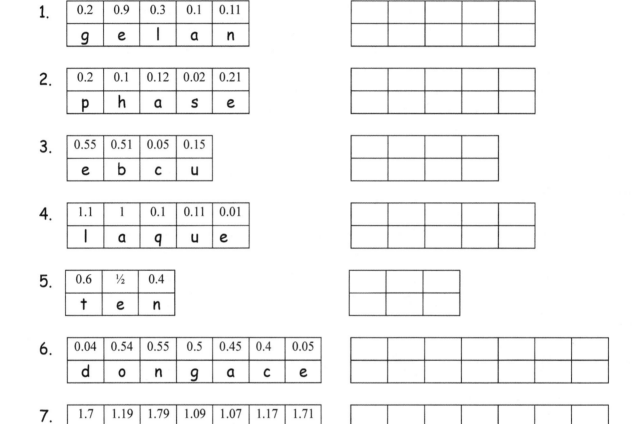

1.

0.2	0.9	0.3	0.1	0.11
g	e	l	a	n

2.

0.2	0.1	0.12	0.02	0.21
p	h	a	s	e

3.

0.55	0.51	0.05	0.15
e	b	c	u

4.

1.1	1	0.1	0.11	0.01
l	a	q	u	e

5.

0.6	½	0.4
t	e	n

6.

0.04	0.54	0.55	0.5	0.45	0.4	0.05
d	o	n	g	a	c	e

7.

1.7	1.19	1.79	1.09	1.07	1.17	1.71
g	e	r	n	i	t	e

8.

½	¼	0.8	0.2	¾	0.3
b	u	r	n	e	m

9.

0.4	⅓	¼	0.1	½
p	a	r	g	h

**Write out the first letter of each of your words.
You should get another mathematical word!**

Sums and Differences with Fractions

The **sum** of two numbers is found by adding them.

The **difference** of two numbers is found by subtracting the smallest from the largest.

Work out the missing numbers in the following grids like this:

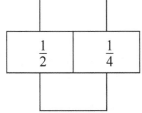

← The sum of the two numbers goes here $(3\frac{1}{2})$

← The difference of the two numbers goes here $(2\frac{1}{2})$

1.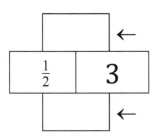

2.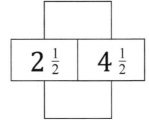

3.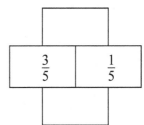

4.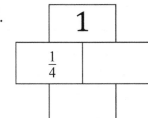

5.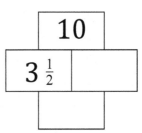

6.

7.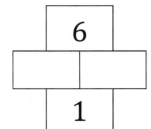

8.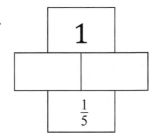

9.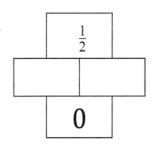

Equivalent Pairs

Cut out the following squares

Match them so that each pair of adjacent sides have equal amounts.

	$\frac{3}{4}$			$\frac{3}{20}$			0.03	
$\frac{1}{10}$	A	50%	80%	B	1.5%	1	C	$\frac{1}{4}$
	$\frac{1}{5}$			$\frac{2}{5}$			$\frac{1}{8}$	
	$\frac{1}{3}$			0.05			0.005	
6%	D	1%	0.5	E	$\frac{4}{5}$	0.6	F	7%
	0.75			3%			0.15	
	40%			0.2			0.02	
25%	G	0.55	0.7	H	100%	0.01	I	$\frac{3}{5}$
	0.3			0.08			5%	

Percentages Dominoes

Cut out the dominoes cards and fit them together so that they form a closed loop.

12	50% of 6

5.5	10% of 50

2	25% of 40

6	10% of 15

4	50% of 11

8	25% of 24

10.5	100% of 8

3	10% of 40

20	5% of 40

5	50% of 21

10	20% of 60

1.5	20% of 100

Fraction Action

- This is a game for 2-3 players

- Take it in turns to throw two 1 to 6 dice and multiply the two numbers together.

- Now pick a fraction from the 'Fraction Box' and find this fraction of your number. Find your result on the playing grid and shade it in your colour.

- If you can't find the result or it has already been shaded then that is the end of your turn.

- The winner is the first player to get a line of 4 (horizontal, vertical or diagonal).

Fraction Box

$\frac{1}{2}$	$\frac{1}{3}$	$\frac{2}{3}$
$\frac{1}{4}$	$\frac{3}{4}$	$\frac{1}{5}$

Playing Grid

12	5	2	8	1
10	1	24	12	4
6	2	4	15	9
18	16	9	6	3
5	8	3	20	10

Run a Mile!

A PE teacher times his class running a mile. Use the clues to work out the times for each pupil and write in their names .

6min 58sec	5min 59sec	6min 45sec	6min 19sec	5min 45sec
_____	_____	_____	_____	_____

5min 30sec	6min 8sec	5min 8sec	5min 31 sec	6min 15sec
_____	_____	_____	_____	_____

6min 30 sec	7min 4sec	6min 1sec	6min 20sec	6min 40sec
_____	_____	_____	_____	_____

6min 35sec	5min 10sec	5min 55sec	7min 19sec	5min 50sec
_____	_____	_____	_____	_____

- Will was the fastest.
- Dan was the slowest.
- Alice ran the mile in $5\frac{1}{2}$ minutes.
- Wendy was 1 minute slower than the fastest runner.
- Diran ran the mile in $6\frac{1}{2}$ minutes.
- Oscar ran the mile in $6\frac{1}{4}$ minutes.
- Henry was 58 seconds faster than Wendy.
- Izzy ran the mile in $5\frac{3}{4}$ minutes.
- Shaz was 25 seconds faster than Oscar.
- Tiana finished 37 seconds before Wendy.
- Emily finished half a minute after Tiana.

- Rupert was 20 seconds slower than Helena.
- Helena was 2 seconds faster than Emily.
- Tim was faster than Helena, but slower than Shaz.
- Lola ran the mile in 380 seconds.
- Ortise was 21 seconds faster than Dan.
- Rachel was 6 seconds slower than Ortise.
- Ellie took 70 seconds longer than Alice.
- Ronnie was 44 seconds faster than the slowest member of the class.
- Cath ran the mile in $6\frac{3}{4}$ minutes.

Write out the names from fastest to slowest. The first letter of each name should spell out a question for you to answer.

Pupil Places

Miss Smith's class are seated around 3 tables as shown below. Use the clues to work out who is sitting in which place.

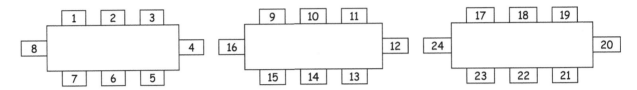

- Asha sits opposite George. Their numbers add to 40. Asha's number is 6 less than George's

- Nita, Cara and Mo sit in a row. Their numbers multiply to give 990. Cara's number is even. Mo's number is the greatest of the three.

- Paul sits opposite Alice. Alice's number is 3 times Paul's.

- Sinead sits next to Dan. Their numbers multiply to give 210. Sinead's number is odd.

- Rachel sits opposite Will. Rachel's number is half of Will's.

- Bob sits opposite Mia. Mia's number is an even multiple of 11.

- Tasha's number is found by squaring Rachel's number.

- Sue's number is a third of Annie's. Their numbers add to 28.

- Lee's number is in both the 4 and 5 times tables.

- David and Sam sit on the same table. Their numbers add to 43. Sam's number is odd.

- Mick's number is a quarter of Max's.

- Bea's number has only 1 factor.

- Joe's number is found by doubling Tim's number and then adding Mick's number.

Left...... Right......

Work out the easy question on the left and then use your answer to help you work out the more difficult question on the right.

1.	300 + 400 =	299 + 398 =
2.	1000 - 200 =	1000 - 195 =
3.	7 × £2 =	7 × £1.99 =
4.	£6 + £4 =	£5.99 + £3.99 =
5.	£100 - £20 =	£100 - £19.95 =
6.	2^2 =	20^2 =
7.	2 × 3 × 4 =	20 × 30 × 40 =
8.	4 + 5 =	3.9 + 4.9 =
9.	3.7 - 2 =	3.7 - 1.9 =
10.	100 ÷ 10 =	100 ÷ 5 =

Use the methods you have learnt to work out these:

    a. 199 + 599   b. 3 × £2.99   c. £200 - £3.99

    d. 30^2 e. 13.6 - 2.9   f. 3000 ÷ 5

Answers

Speedy Sums

1. 489, CAB
2. 483, CAR
3. 1671, SKIS
4. 9085, BOAT
5. 4835, CART
6. 9762, BIKE
7. 53762, TRIKE
8. 168521, SKATES

3, 2, 1, …..

A.
1. 321, 231, 123, 213
2. 132 or 312
3. 123, 132, 213, 231, 312, 321
4. 321
5. 123

B.
1. 321 – 123 = 198
2. 891
3. 198 + 891 = 1089

C.
1. 863 – 368 = 495
2. 594
4. 495 + 594 = 1089

D. Answers will always be 1089 (if the difference in qu 1 is 99, think of it as 099)

Challenge: Yes, you get the answer 10890: the whole nuumber has to be reflected at stage 2, so 1234 would become 4321.

Decimal Sums and Differences

Answers are shaded. In questions 6, 7, 8, 9 answers may be either way round.

1.
	7.6	
1.5		6.1
	4.6	

2.
	4.3	
2.4		1.9
	0.5	

3.
	12.1	
6.3		5.8
	0.5	

4.
	10	
2.3		7.7
	5.4	

5.
	5.4	
4.9		0.5
	4.4	

6.
	1	
0.4		0.6
	0.2	

7.
	1	
0.2		0.8
	0.6	

8.
	2	
1.5		0.5
	1	

9.
	3	
1.9		1.1
	0.8	

Routes Home

Ed: 1.2, 1.4, 1.6, 1.8, 2, 2.2, 2.4, 2.6

Jo: 1.1, 1.4, 1.7, 2, 2.3, 2.6, 2.9, 3.2, 3.5, 3.8

Tim: 2.9, 2.6, 2.3, 2, 1.7, 1.4, 1.1, 0.8, 0.5, 0.2

Amy   0.9, 1.9, 2.9, 3.9, 4.9, 5.9

Sue: 1.5, 1.9, 2.3, 2.7, 3.1, 3.5

Challenge: There are an infinite number of answers. Here are a few:

(2.5, 2.7, 2.9, 3.1, 3.3, 3.5, 3.7, 3.9, 4.1, 4.3, 4.5, 4.7, 4.9)

(2.5, 2.9, 3.3, 3.7, 4.1, 4.5, 4.9) (2.5, 3.1, 3.7, 4.3, 4.9)

Decimal Arrows

A.

9.4	→	12	→	14.6		17.2	→	19.8		→	+2.6
↑		↑		↑		↑		↑			
8.3	→	10.9	→	13.5	→	16.1	→	18.7		↑	+1.1
↑		↑		↑		↑		↑			
7.2	→	9.8	→	12.4	→	15	→	17.6			
↑		↑		↑		↑		↑			
6.1	→	8.7	→	11.3	→	13.9	→	16.5			
↑		↑		↑		↑		↑			
5	→	7.6	→	10.2	→	12.8	→	15.4			

B.

8.3	→	12.8	→	17.3	→	21.8	→	26.3		→	+4.5
↑		↑		↑		↑		↑			
7.4	→	11.9	→	16.4	→	20.9	→	25.4		↑	+0.9
↑		↑		↑		↑		↑			
6.5	→	11	→	15.5	→	20	→	24.5			
↑		↑		↑		↑		↑			
5.6	→	10.1	→	14.6	→	19.1	→	23.6			
↑		↑		↑		↑		↑			
4.7	→	9.2	→	13.7	→	18.2	→	22.7			

Make a Metre

The correct arrangement is:
C F E
I H B
D A G

Wizard Maze

The answers to each question are shown below. The way out is at number 9.

5 → -1 → 2 → -5 → -6 → -3 → 4 → -4 → -14 → -9 → 1 → -8 → -13 → -2 → 8 → -10 → -12 → 3 → -7 → -16 → -12 → -1 → 19 → -11 → 9

Set the Table

A.

×	6	8	9	5
7	42	56	63	35
2	12	16	18	10
4	24	32	36	20
3	18	24	27	15

B.

×	4	3	9	7
2	8	6	18	14
5	20	15	45	35
6	24	18	54	42
8	32	24	72	56

C.

×	7	9	5	3
2	14	18	10	6
8	56	72	40	24
4	28	36	20	12
6	42	54	30	18

Challenge: All the numbers are even. The numbers along the top are odd and the numbers along the left are even. So each number is the product of an odd and an even number, which must be even.

Number Properties

11	46	68	51	26	38	90	33	27	47	22
31	25	52	70	21	56	41	15	24	10	65
55	64	39	42	76	22	43	2	48	12	34
61	36	53	14	84	63	78	30	80	8	62
32	9	75	23	82	7	13	6	18	3	66
18	16	33	35	77	28	59	40	5	20	23
45	17	37	13	50	72	44	26	19	69	17

↑ blue   ↑ red   ↑ green

The answer is 150.

Factors of 150: 1, 2, 3, 5, 6, 10, 15, 25, 30, 50, 75, 150

Challenge: 1 and 4 could have been shaded green or blue
49 could have been shaded red or blue

1 to 9 Puzzle

The order does not matter in these questions.

A. Pupils should be encouraged to consider the factors of the 3 results. This will tell them if there are any numbers which can only go in one place. Using this method, 7 and 8 must go in the middle calculation, meaning that the remaining number must be 1. 5 must go in the top calculation because the result ends in '0'.

$4 \times 5 \times 9 = 180$ $1 \times 7 \times 8 = 56$ $2 \times 3 \times 6 = 36$

B. 5 must go in the middle calculation, 7 must go in the third calculation and all three numbers must be odd as the result is odd.

$2 \times 4 \times 8 = 64$ $3 \times 5 \times 6 = 90$ $1 \times 7 \times 9 = 63$

C. 5 and 7 must go in the top calculation, so the remaining number must be 3.

$3 \times 5 \times 7 = 105$ $1 \times 4 \times 6 = 24$ $2 \times 8 \times 9 = 144$

Make a Name

1. 842, MAT
4. 268, TIM
7. 1884, EMMA

2. 213, TED
5. 2694, TINA
8. 4991, ANNE

3. 485, AMY
6. 208, TOM

Divide Again

1. $239 \div 5 = 47$ rem 4	2. $518 \div 8 = 64$ rem 6	3. $2446 \div 9 = 271$ rem 7
$47 \div 4 = 11$ rem 3	$64 \div 6 = 10$ rem 4	$271 \div 7 = 38$ rem 5
$11 \div 3 = 3$ rem 2	$10 \div 4 = 2$ rem 2	$38 \div 5 = 7$ rem 3
$3 \div 2 = 1$ rem 1	$2 \div 2 = 1$ rem 0	$7 \div 3 = 2$ rem 1

Pupils should notice a pattern occurring with the remainders. Instead of giving pupils the answer, you could ask them to spot a pattern with the remainders. If they can give you the correct pattern, they should have the right answers.

Times Ten

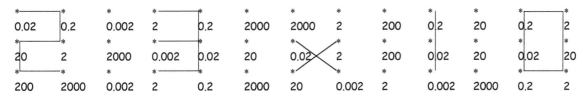

The result is 23 × 10 so the answer is 230.

That's an Order!

1.
0.1	0.11	0.2	0.3	0.9
a	n	g	l	e

2.
0.02	0.1	0.12	0.2	0.21
s	h	a	p	e

3.
0.05	0.15	0.51	0.55
c	u	b	e

4.
0.01	0.1	0.11	1	1.1
e	q	u	a	l

5.
0.4	½	0.6
n	e	t

6.
0.04	0.05	0.4	0.45	0.5	0.54	0.55
d	e	c	a	g	o	n

7.
1.07	1.09	1.17	1.19	1.7	1.71	1.79
i	n	t	e	g	e	r

8.
0.2	¼	0.3	½	¾	0.8
n	u	m	b	e	r

9.
0.1	¼	⅓	0.4	½
g	r	a	p	h

The first letter of each of the words spell 'ascending'.

Sums and Differences with Fractions

Answers are shaded. In questions 7, 8, 9 answers may be either way round.

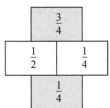

4.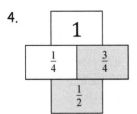

5.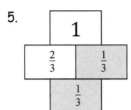

6.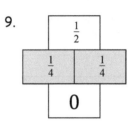

7.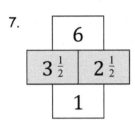

8.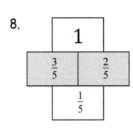

9.

Equivalent Pairs

The correct arrangement is: D I F
                                    A E B
                                    H C G

Percentage Dominoes

50% of 6 = 3 → 10% of 40 = 4 → 50% of 11 = 5.5 → 10% of 50 = 5 → 50% of 21 = 10.5 →
100% of 8 = 8 → 25% of 24 = 6 → 10% of 15 = 1.5 → 20% of 100 = 20 → 5% of 40 = 2 →
25% of 40 = 10 → 20% of 60 = 12

Run a Mile!

5min 8sec Will	5min 10sec Henry	5min 30sec Alice	5min 31sec Tiana	5min 45sec Izzy
5min 50sec Shaz	5min 55sec Tim	5min 59sec Helena	6min 1 sec Emily	6min 8sec Wendy
6min 15sec Oscar	6min 19sec Rupert	6min 20sec Lola	6min 30sec Diran	6min 35sec Ronnie
6min 40sec Ellie	6min 45sec Cath	6min 58sec Ortise	7min 4sec Rachel	7min 19sec Dan

The first letter of each name spells out the question: 'What is the World Record?'

At the time of writing the men's record holder is Hicham El Guerrouj (3mins 43.13 secs) and the women's record holder is Svetlana Masterkova (4mins 12.56secs).

Pupil Places

1 Bea	2 Paul	3 Mick	4 Rachel
5 Tim	6 Alice	7 Sue	8 Will
9 Nita	10 Cara	11 Mo	12 Max
13 Joe	14 Dan	15 Sinead	16 Tasha
17 Asha	18 Bob	19 Sam	20 Lee
21 Annie	22 Mia	23 George	24 David

Left…… Right……

This activity practices a really important skill: Using a known answer to help you work out a more difficult calculation. I would encourage plenty of class discussion and work in pairs or groups, to help pupils become aware of the different methods and 'tricks', which can be used.

1.	$300 + 400 = 700$	$299 + 398 = 697$	299 is 1 less than 300, 398 is 2 less than 400, so the answer will be 3 less than 700.
2.	$1000 - 200 = 800$	$1000 - 195 = 805$	5 less is being subtracted, so the answer will be 5 more.
3.	$7 \times £2 = £14$	$7 \times £1.99 = £13.93$	£1.99 is 1p less than £2, so the answer will be $7 \times 1p$ less.
4.	$£6 + £4 = £10$	$£5.99 + £3.99 = £9.98$	£5.99 and £3.99 are each 1p less than £6 and £4 resp. So answer will be 2p less.
5.	$£100 - £20 = £80$	$£100 - £19.95 = £80.05$	£19.95 is 5p less than £20, so answer will be 5p more.
6.	$2^2 = 4$	$20^2 = 400$	$2 \times 2 = 4$, so $20 \times 20 = 400$ (100 times greater)
7.	$2 \times 3 \times 4 = 24$	$20 \times 30 \times 40 = 24000$	Answer will be 1000× greater, as each value is 10× greater and $10 \times 10 \times 10 = 1000$
8.	$4 + 5 = 9$	$3.9 + 4.9 = 8.8$	Each value is 0.1 less, so answer will be 0.2 less.
9.	$3.7 - 2 = 1.7$	$3.7 - 1.9 = 1.8$	1.9 is 0.1 less than 2, so 0.1 less is being subtracted. Answer will be 0.1 greater.
10.	$100 \div 10 = 10$	$100 \div 5 = 20$	Answer will be double as you are dividing it into a number which is half as large.

	Answer	Easy calculation to be used
a.	798	200 + 600
b.	£8.97	3 × £3
c.	£196.01	£200 - £4
d.	900	3^2
e.	10.7	13.6 - 3
f.	600	3000 ÷ 10

Lightning Source UK Ltd.
Milton Keynes UK
UKOW07f2349031116

286854UK00012B/471/P